Animals Helping People

by Suzanne Venino

A young boy drives camels across a desert in Africa.

BOOKS FOR YOUNG EXPLORERS
NATIONAL GEOGRAPHIC SOCIETY

For thousands of years people have used animals to help them with their work. Some animals give us food or clothing. Animals help people in many different ways.

A cowboy herds horses through snow toward a corral to be fed. Cowboys work on ranches where they tend horses and cattle. Riding a horse helps a cowboy do his job.

ROBBERS ROOST RANCH, MONTANA

Riding a horse can make learning easier for children with special problems. These children are making friends with a gentle pony. Her name is Coconut. Grown-ups lead the pony and tell Kristen how to sit in the saddle. Donna learns to balance and use the reins. John gives Coconut a pat.

ABOVE: THAILAND; BELOW: TUNISIA

Camels race down a sandy slope. Riding camels was once the only way people could travel long distances across the Sahara. Now people can drive over the desert sand in jeeps and trucks. But in many places, animals are still used for transportation today. In Africa, a young boy rides a donkey through a field of flowers. A boy in Asia rides a water buffalo. Turn the page to see another kind of animal that people ride.

It's a parade! Each year on the Asian island of Sri Lanka, there is a big parade with as many as 80 elephants.

The elephants march through the streets wearing colorful capes, bright jewels, and bells. Thousands of people come to watch. Have you ever seen elephants in a parade? Have you ever been to a circus?

KANDY, SRI LANKA

Animals trained to carry heavy loads on their backs are called
pack animals. On a camping trip in Montana, horses and
a mule carry food, tents, sleeping bags, and other supplies.

Camels have wide, tough feet. They can walk on hot sand, and travel many miles without eating or drinking. In some desert lands, people still use camels to carry goods to market.

With their tusks and trunks, elephants move heavy logs in the forests of Southeast Asia.

Elephants are very strong and can be trained to do many jobs. Trainers ride the elephants and shout commands as they work. The trainers also make sure that the elephants rest and get plenty of food to eat.

THAILAND

SRI LANKA

Using its trunk like a hose,
an elephant takes a shower
to cool off after working in
the hot sun. On its way to work,
another elephant carries food for
its lunch. Elephants eat leaves,
roots, grass, fruit, and tree bark.
Working elephants often eat
about 300 pounds of food a day!

Isn't this a strange pair? A camel and a donkey pull a plow through a field in Africa.

Today, many farmers have tractors and other big machines to work their fields. But in many places, farmers still use animals. In Asia, an ox-drawn plow cuts through a wet rice field. On a farm in Europe, two horses pull a harrow to break up the soil.

ABOVE: MOROCCO; BELOW: SOUTH KOREA

Near the North Pole, a team of dogs pulls an explorer's sled. They are crossing the ice of the frozen Arctic Ocean. Sled dogs must be strong and able to work in a very cold climate. Such dogs have thick fur that keeps them warm.

Horses haul a sleigh over snow-covered hills in Vermont.
The men are collecting sap from maple trees.

They pour the sap into a large tank on the sleigh.
Later the sap will be boiled and made into maple syrup.

Nine-year-old Clay runs
with his horse, Lisa,
to give her some exercise.
Clay takes good care of Lisa.

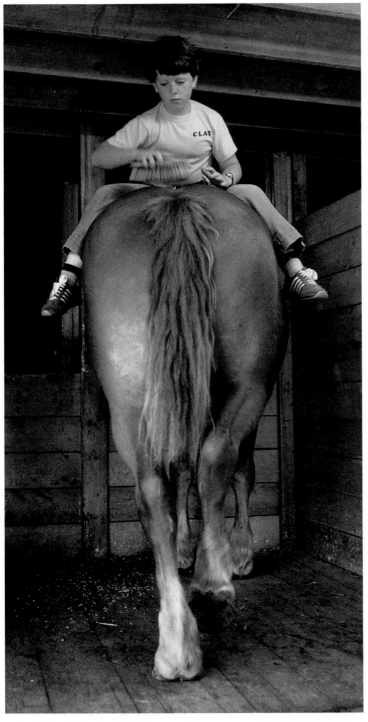

Clay sits on Lisa's back
to brush her coat.
He also feeds her and
cleans out her stall.

On the Idaho farm where
Clay lives, Lisa helps do
the chores. She is trained
to pull a cart, and to team
with another horse
to haul a large hay wagon.
She can also be ridden.
Lisa is much more than
just a work horse, though.
Lisa is Clay's friend.

In the mountains of California, these dogs are being trained to find people who may be lost or hurt.

Each dog wears a bright vest to show that it belongs to a search team. Dogs have a good sense of smell. Sniffing the ground and air, they can follow a person's scent.

YOSEMITE NATIONAL PARK, CALIFORNIA

Here, a man makes believe he is hurt. When the rescue dog finds him, the trainer uses a radio to call for help.

Many children like to keep animals as pets. This young boy puts his rabbits back into their cage. Rabbits are friendly and fun to play with.

Children who have pets must learn to take care of them. They must be sure that the pet has food and water every day, and a clean, warm place to live.

A tiny hamster nibbles on carrots and celery. A young girl gives her kitten a hug. Pets often become special companions.

In wintertime, a sheep's wool coat grows very thick.
In the spring, a Navajo woman shears the wool from a sheep.
The animal lies very still. Shearing does not hurt the sheep,
and its coat will grow back. The shorn wool can be spun into yarn.
The yarn is woven into blankets and clothing.

ABOVE: NAVAJO INDIAN RESERVATION, ARIZONA; BELOW: NEAR GREEN SPRINGS, WYOMING

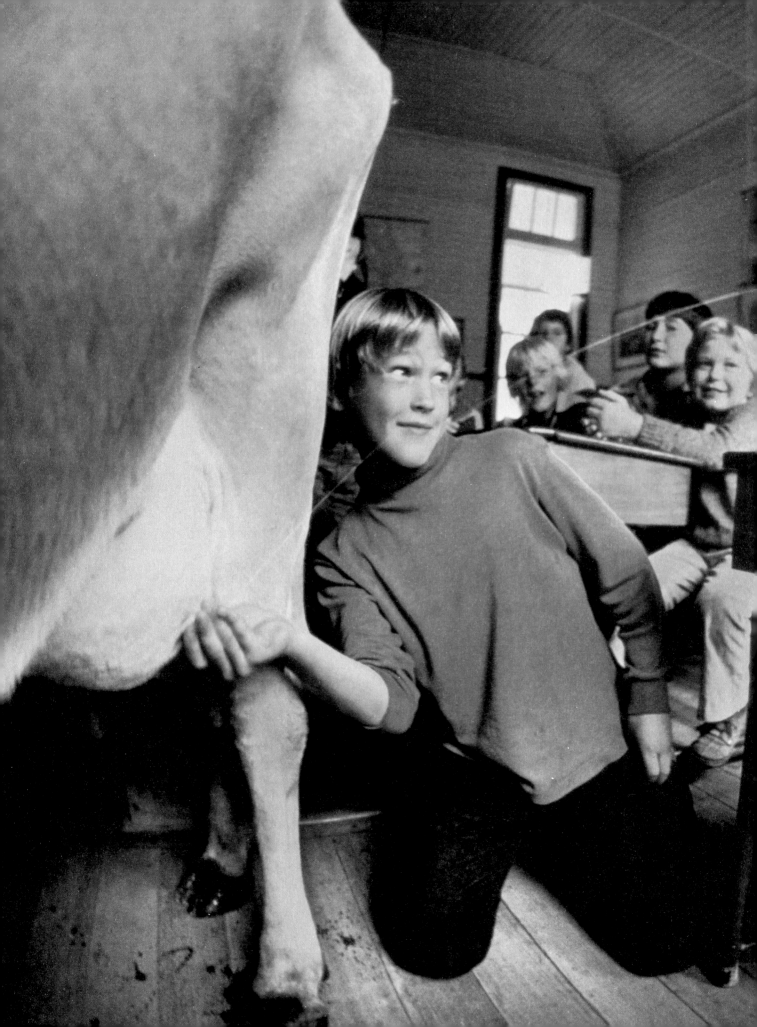

LEFT: KORUMBURRA PRIMARY SCHOOL, VICTORIA, AUSTRALIA;
BELOW: SEQUIM GAME FARM, OLYMPIC PENINSULA, WASHINGTON

What a shot! A boy squirts milk into the mouth of a classmate. This cow has been brought to school for a class on farm animals.

On a farm, a girl milks a goat. Many farm animals give us food or clothing. Other animals help people work. Some animals make good pets. Look around you: Can you find some other ways that animals help you?

31

A donkey pulls a milk cart along a country lane in Ireland.

Cover: A team of horses hauls a wagon piled high with hay on a farm in Idaho.

Endpapers: A traveler and his pony carry supplies up a mountain in northern India.

Published by
   The National Geographic Society
Gilbert M. Grosvenor, *President*
Melvin M. Payne, *Chairman of the Board*
Owen R. Anderson, *Executive Vice President*
Robert L. Breeden, *Vice President,*
   Publications and Educational Media

Prepared by
   The Special Publications Division
Donald J. Crump, *Director*
Philip B. Silcott, *Associate Director*
William L. Allen, William R. Gray, *Assistant*
   Directors

Staff for this Book
Merrill Windsor, *Managing Editor*
David P. Johnson, *Picture Editor*
Cynthia B. Scudder, *Art Director*
Monica P. Bradsher, *Consulting Editor*
Gail N. Hawkins, *Researcher*
Rebecca Bittle Johns, *Illustrations Assistant*
Nancy F. Berry, Pamela A. Black, Mary Frances
   Brennan, Mary Elizabeth Davis, Rosamund
   Garner, Victoria D. Garrett, Virginia W.
   McCoy, Cleo E. Petroff, Tammy Presley, Sheryl
   A. Prohovich, Carol A. Rocheleau, Kathleen
   T. Shea, *Staff Assistants*

Engraving, Printing, and Product Manufacture
Robert W. Messer, *Manager*
George V. White, *Production Manager*
Mary A. Bennett, *Production Project Manager*
Mark R. Dunlevy, Richard A. McClure, David
   V. Showers, Gregory Storer, *Assistant*
   Production Managers
Katherine H. Donohue, *Senior Production*
   Assistant
Julia F. Warner, *Production Staff Assistant*

Consultants
Dr. Glenn O. Blough, Dr. Janet Brennan, Susan Stanford, *Educational Consultants*
Lynda Ehrlich, *Reading Consultant*
Dr. Michael W. Fox, Scientific Director, The Humane Society
   of the United States; Dr. Henry W. Setzer, Curator of Mammals,
   Emeritus, Smithsonian Institution; Michael J. Walker, Author,
   WILD ANIMALS THAT HELP PEOPLE, *Scientific Consultants*

Illustrations Credits
Chris Pietsch (cover); Thomas J. Abercrombie, NGS Staff (front and back endpapers, 10-11 lower); Fiore/EXPLORER (1); Jonathan Blair (2-3); Susan McElhinney (4 upper, 4 lower, 5); Cliff Hollenbeck (6 upper); NGS Photographer David Alan Harvey (6 lower); NGS Photographer W. Robert Moore (6-7); Dieter and Mary Plage/BRUCE COLEMAN LTD. (8-9); Tom and Pat Leeson (10-11 upper, 31 right); David Austen/BLACK STAR (12-13); Dilip Mehta/CONTACT PRESS IMAGES (14, 14-15); G. Zawadski/EXPLORER (16); Christian Zuber/BRUCE COLEMAN LTD. (16-17); A. Le Toquin/EXPLORER (17); Ira Block (18-19); NGS Photographer George F. Mobley (18 upper); NGS Photographer Emory Kristof (20-21); Christopher R. Anderson (22, 23 left, 23 upper right); David Falconer (24, 25 lower left, 25 right); Ken Sherman/BRUCE COLEMAN INC. (26 left); ANIMALS ANIMALS/Zig Leszczynski (26 upper right); Walter Chandoha (27); Annie Griffiths (28-29); John Running/BLACK STAR (29); John Lamb/DITLA (30-31); Adam Woolfit (32).

Library of Congress CIP Data

Venino, Suzanne, 1953-
   Animals helping people.

   (Books for young explorers)
   Summary: Briefly describes some of the many tasks that animals perform and other ways in which they benefit people.
   1. Working animals—Juvenile literature. [1. Working animals] I. Title. II. Series.
SF172.V45 1983   636.08'86   83-13184
ISBN 0-87044-488-3 (regular edition)
ISBN 0-87044-493-X (library edition)